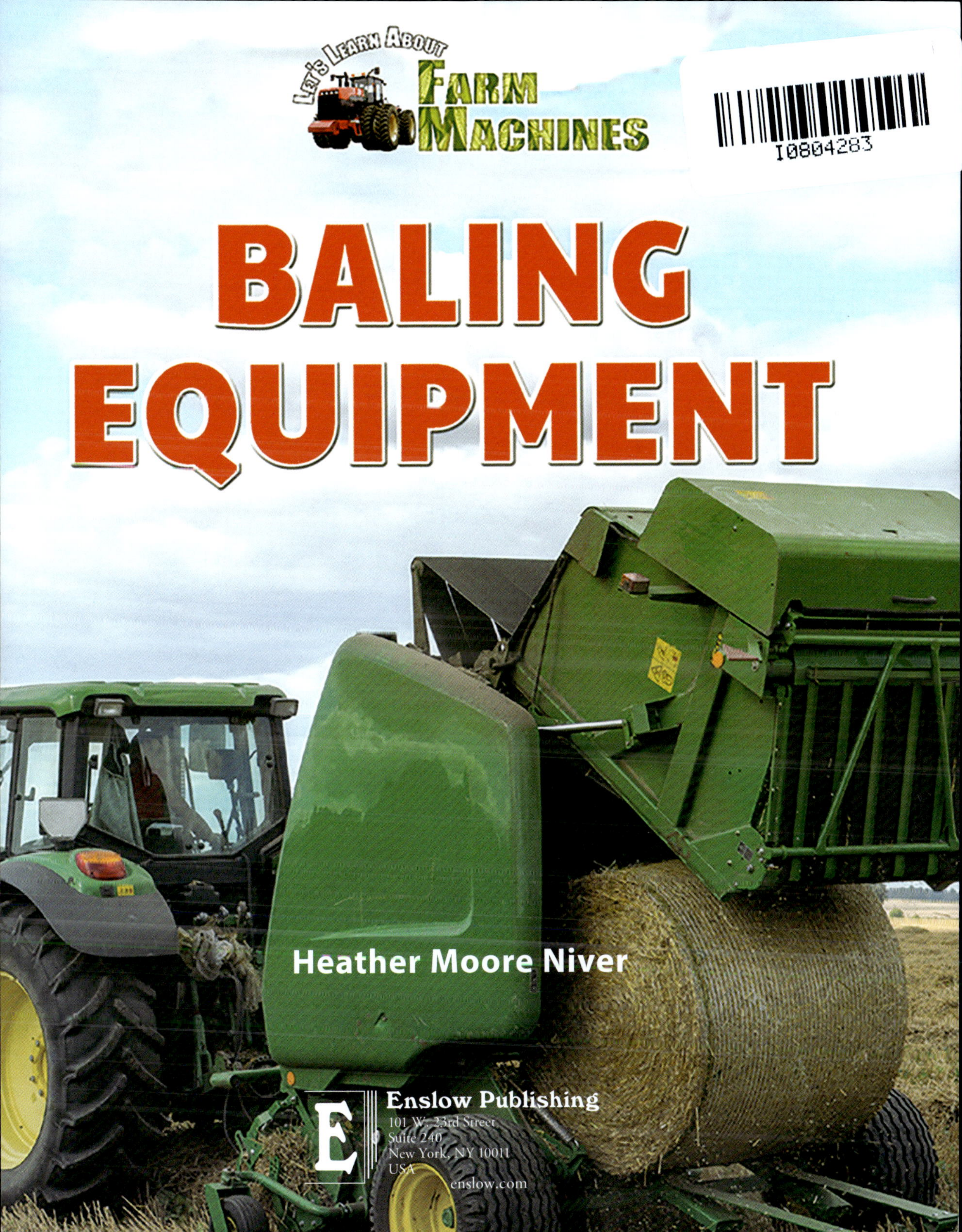

Let's Learn About Farm Machines

BALING EQUIPMENT

Heather Moore Niver

Enslow Publishing
101 W. 23rd Street
Suite 240
New York, NY 10011
USA
enslow.com

Words to Know

alfalfa A plant with flowers. It is sometimes made into hay.

bale A bunch of something, like dried grasses, held together with twine.

bind To press together.

circular Like a circle.

harobed A machine that picks up bales of hay and stacks them.

plunger A machine used to press hay into a bale.

steel A very strong metal made from iron.

CONTENTS

Farms need lots of hay bales to feed their animals.

Oh, Hay!

On a farm, bales of hay are important. Animals like cows and sheep eat hay. Hay is made from dry grass and plants. A baler shapes hay into bales.

Fast Fact

Hay can be made of grass, alfalfa, or other plants.

This alfalfa has been cut down. It will become hay when it dries.

Planting and Cutting

Farmers plant grass or alfalfa. A mowing machine cuts it down when it is still green. It also breaks the hay. Then the grass is raked into long rows.

FAST FACT
The mower cuts hay and breaks it into smaller pieces the animals can eat.

A farmer drives a tractor with a hay baler.

Baling Time

The grass dries in the field. A hay baler scoops it up. It presses the hay into a bale. It uses a machine called a **plunger**. The plunger also cuts the ends of the bales.

FAST FACT

Balers are made out of different kids of **steel**.

Hay bales are tied and tossed into a wagon.

Tied in Twine

Balers tie string or twine around each bale. This keeps the hay together. It takes about two seconds to bind and tie each bale. Then the bale is dropped to the ground.

FAST FACT

Some balers have a machine called a kicker. It kicks the bales into a hay rack.

A round baler creates large bales of hay.

Round Balers

A round baler has two circular blades. They pick up hay. The hay is rolled into a round shape. When the baler is full, the bale rolls out the back.

FAST FACT

Round hay bales can weigh 800 to 2,000 pounds (363 to 907 kilograms).

A tractor uses a bale mover to lift a large bale of hay.

Round Bales

Tractors use equipment called a bale mover. It carries round bales. Bale movers have spikes. The spikes stab through the round bale. Then the heavy bale can be lifted.

FAST FACT

Round bales can be kept outside. Rain rolls off their round sides.

A farmer stacks square hay bales.

Square It Up

Some farmers like to make square bales. They are smaller and much lighter than round bales. One person can pick up a square bale.

FAST FACT
Square bales are really rectangular.

The PTO takes the power from the tractor and connects to the baler so it can run.

Baler Power!

A tractor pulls the baler. The baler is connected to the tractor. This is how it gets power. The PTO, or power takeoff, does this job.

FAST FACT

Balers have special wide tires that don't damage the hay.

Farmers use machines like this one to pick up bales from the field.

Pick 'Em Up!

Finally, farmers need to pick up the hay bales. They use a harobed or bale wagon. It picks up and stacks bales.

Activity

Make Your Own Hay

Time to make your own square hay bale!

YOU WILL NEED:

- Brown paper bag
- Brown construction paper
- Glue
- Scissors

Step 1: Cut brown paper into thin strips.

Step 2: Crumple the strips.

Step 3: Cover one side of the bag at a time with glue.

Step 4: Press crumpled paper on the bag. Repeat on each side until all sides of the bag are covered.

You have made a square bale of hay!

Learn More

Books

Bell, Samantha. *Baler*. Ann Arbor, MI: Cherry Lake Publishing, 2017.

Berne, Emma Carlson. *Balers Go to Work*. Minneapolis, MN: Lerner Publications, 2018.

Mihaly, Christy. *Hey, Hey, Hay! A Tale of Bales and the Machines that Make Them*. New York, NY: Holiday House, 2018.

Websites

John Deere Kids
www.deere.com/en/connect-with-john-deere/john-deere-for-kids/
Learn about farm equipment, safety, and more!

Tractors for Kids – Learn Farm Vehicles and Equipment with Blippi
www.youtube.com/watch?v=ZyEnVLPhjUc
Check out tractors hay balers, and other equipment in action!

Index

Published in 2020 by Enslow Publishing, LLC.

101 W. 23rd Street, Suite 240, New York, NY 10011

Library of Congress Cataloging-in-Publication Data

Names: Niver, Heather Moore, author.
Title: Baling equipment / Heather Moore Niver.
Description: New York : Enslow Publishing, 2020. | Series: Let's learn about farm machines | Includes bibliographical references and index. | Audience: Grades K-3.
Identifiers: LCCN 2019010202| ISBN 9781978513075 (library bound) | ISBN 9781978513051 (pbk.) | ISBN 9781978513068 (6 pack)
Subjects: LCSH: Agricultural machinery--Juvenile literature. Baling--Juvenile literature.
Classification: LCC S675.25 .N58 2020 | DDC 631.3--dc23

LC record available at https://lccn.loc.gov/2019010202
Printed in the United States of America

Photos Credits: Cover, pp. 1, 12, interior pages background landscape Jurgis Mankauskas/Shutterstock.com; p. 4 2ndLookGraphics/iStock/Getty Images; pp. 5, 7, 9, 11, 13, 15, 17, 19, 22 (hay bale) photomaster/Shutterstock.com; p. 6 BanksPhotos/iStock/Getty Images; p. 8 © iStockphoto.com/SimplyCreativePhotography; p. 10 FLPA/Alamy Stock Photo; p. 14 All Canada Photos/Alamy Stock Photo; p. 16 Tetra Images, LLC/Alamy Stock Photo; p. 18 © iStockphoto.com/Richardsugden; p. 20 KaeCsImages/Shutterstock.com; p. 23 solidcolours/iStock/Getty Images; cover, p. 1 logo element (tractor) Krivosheev Vitaly/Shutterstock.com.